CN01583836

# Poems for the Internet

Volume 2

By

Clive Brookes

First Edition

Copyright © 2008 Clive Brookes
First published in Great Britain 2008.
All rights reserved.
Published by Timepiece publications.

Edgehill
Rock Hill, Mansfield,
Notts NG28 2JP.
England.

Printed by Portshel Industries,
Portland College
Nottingham Road,
Mansfield,
Notts NG18 4TJ
Tel (01623) 491255
Fax (01623) 491631

Front cover designed by
Peter Olley Design,
Willow Tree Cottage,
Woodhouse Lane,
Skegby, Sutton in Ashfield,
Notts NG17 3BZ.
Tel (01623) 441193
Fax (01623) 555097

This book is dedicated to everyone and everything including friends of the "White Crow Poetry Forum" on the internet, which has ever inspired me. But it is especially dedicated to my darling wife Patricia.

Thanks are due to various magazines and journals, newspapers etc where some of these poems or slightly different versions have appeared. Thanks are also due to Portshel Industries for their invaluable help with the production of this book.

Special thanks to Carrie Austin
for proof reading and editing.
My further thanks to everyone who has helped
with the promotion of this book.

## Introduction

Clive Brookes is a retired merchant seaman. He is well known for his prize-winning poetry, particularly on the subject of life in the North Sea oil fields. Many of Clive's works have been published in numerous books, magazines, newspapers etc, and also recited on television and radio.

In contrast to his life at sea, Clive is a family man and landowner with a great love of the countryside. His interests are many and varied ranging from sport to the arts and antiques.

Clive has seen and experienced much of life at first hand, which is reflected in his poetry. To quote him "I have travelled more by shanks's pony than by Rolls". This is Clive's third book of poems and most of the poems in this book have been written over the last three years especially for the poetry sites in Cyberspace.

Clive says that the majority of poetry sites on the Internet are a very good way of communicating globally and they give him an insight into the many poetical expressions. Clive like most poets on the internet uses a Pseudonym by which he is well known in the virtual "cafes" he frequents.

**Carrie Austin**

# Contents

# THE BLOODY DOG

My wife thinks more of the dog
than she ever does of me,
when she's watching the Tele'
the dog's sat on the settee.
When we have Sunday lunch
the dam dog gets most 0f the meat,
It doesn't matter when I'm fed
as long as her pet gets to eat.
She grooms, strokes and cuddles it
whilst saying such loving words,
some of the things she says
are expressions I've never heard.
She takes the dog for long walks
and leaves me all on my own.
I wonder if I am the master
or should I be chewing the bone?

## FRESH CREAM CAKES

Close your mind to calories
go on and take a bite,
the cream is so delicious
and the cherry jams just right.
You know you've always liked
the taste of fresh cream cake,
so now have a tasty piece,
what difference will it make?

What difference will it make?
well my mind's in a riot,
part of me says, have a bit
the other "Watch your diet"!

## TO THE POINT ( LIMERICK)

So you think I'm strong and handsome
Whilst I think your cute and curvesome
So now let's entwine
Your body with mine
And that thing called joy, we'll have some.

# THE OLD GARDEN SWING

The movement of the garden swing
is by the wind alone
and grass beneath the seat is dense,
and really overgrown.
The hanging chains are deep in rust
where bright paint used to be,
and the shiny seat where children sat
swinging high and free,
as now become rotten, far beyond repair,
after so many years of such loving care.
All those happy voices within the garden at play
have now grown up, and sadly , moved away.
It's only happy memories that let the swing remain,
as it's no longer safe, too ever use again.

# FOR OUR GLORIOUS REGIMENTS
(VILLANELLE)

We must not let our brave regiments die
It is our duty to protect their fame
And we must tell the people why

Their bravery no one can deny
Great honours in battle they can duly claim
We must not let our old regiments die

We must speak up now and not be shy
Its time our government played the game
And we must tell the public why

Thousands of crosses stand beneath the sky
And many without a warriors name
We must never let our brave regiments die

To their memory, we won't ever say goodbye
Protecting their honour must be our aim
And we must declare the reasons why

Some say "let the past die"
But FREEDOM shouts "it would be a shame"!
We must not let our fine regiments die
And we must tell our young people why.

# TRAFFIC LIGHTS

Whilst waiting at traffic-lights,
something I always do,
is check the car behind
through my mirror's rear view.

I've seen all kinds of faces
expressing every mood,
smiling, sulking, chatting,
anxious and sometimes rude.

These are faces of drivers
travelling near and far,
for all kinds of reasons,
in different makes of car.

No matter how important
their journey happens to be,
until those red lights change
they've got to wait like me.

# FUTURE

Suppose you fall in love with me
and I fall for you,
then I'm sure we'd agree
forever to pursue,
all that lies ahead
forsaking what's behind;
for our pasts we must shed
to nurture "Peace of mind".
This could be the starting line
to set a steady pace,
you with your hand in mine
O! "Let's the future face!"

Onward moving happy feet,
All bridges burnt "Love complete".

## A FEMALE'S RESOLUTION

To overeating I'd become addicted
and my gross state was self inflicted,
at mealtimes I would consume
food until there was no room.
Sweets and ice-cream were a delight
I never thought of cellulite.
weight increased on hips and thighs
'Till clothes I wore were all outsize,
still, on I ate till very soon
my face was like a full moon.
All signs of a girlie figure
disappeared as I got bigger.
Then one day I decided to slim
and get my figure back in trim
through working hard in the gym
and never eating at a whim.
At first it was extremely hard
adhering to the diet card
whilst exercising every day
to help burn the fat away.
Finally I regained my figure
fingers crossed, I'll get no bigger.

# SPRINGTIME DISPLAY

The plum blossom's looking wonderful
kissed by the springtime sun,
and the lovely yellow tulips
proved a planting well done.
The daffodils within stone troughs
nod to each passing breeze,
swaying and reverting
in harmony with the trees.

The snowdrops have all faded,
and the crocuses so gay
dressed in multicolours
have also passed away.
Now hyacinths of pink,
purple, blue and white,
have taken up positions,
such a fragrant delight.

The magnolias this year
have escaped the fearful frost
and every bloom looks wonderful
with not a petal lost.
Come the end of morning frosts
towards the end of May,
in shall go the bedding plants
for the summertime display.

# AN OLD SAILOR DREAMING

Pictures of ships now gone
Which the old salt sailed on,
Set his lonely spirit free
Homeward bound, back to sea.
To tall ships John used to know
More than sixty years ago.
Once again he climbed the masts
Amidst calm, and stormy blasts,
And he saw his shipmate's faces
As they tightened sheets and braces
And visited those dockland places
That have gone except for traces.
How pleased he was to be
In that distant reality,
Until the library clock struck four
Bringing his spirit back ashore

# THE TOLL

I parked my car beneath a sign
warning "Leave within the hour"
but I didn't take notice,
And now, I'm feeling sour
about the ticket on my screen
expressing the council's power.
I didn't intend to be so long
before I drove away,
but I had urgent business
which caused me some delay.
On arriving back at my car
(completely out of breath)
I found the bloody ticket
stating the hour had seen its death.

# LEPRECHAUNS

Those little men in green
Love to take their poteen
They drink it so they say
Nearly all night and day
With guiness in between.

## MURKY NIGHT

The night is wet and foggy,
road signs suddenly appear.
Car rear-lights in a ribbon
round bends disappear.
Neon signs are hazy,
just a mass of coloured light,
suspended in the darkness
of this winter's night.
Brake lights give out warnings
for followers to take heed
that some cars just ahead
are quickly reducing speed.
Noisy blades keep clearing
the cold driving rain,
Oh! how I wish I were
safe back home again.

# MR NORTHERN ROCK

The lady of Threadneedle Street
Said she would give you bail,
To keep Dame Commerce on her feet
And save you going to jail.
You thought you had a Masterplan
That could never fail,
When your enterprise began
On a massive scale.

Now the market's unsteady,
Trembling with each shock.
And all the banks are ready
To desert poor Mr Rock
Who's now awaiting,
"Head upon the Block"

## CANCELLATION

My friends it's the dam Flu
that's keeping me home in my bed,
and every time I sneeze
it rattles the teeth in my head.
My nose is always running
whilst my voice is but a squeak,
I feel the soreness in my throat
whenever I attempt to speak.
My eyes keep on watering
and the sweat it pumps away,
it's put an end to everything
that I'd got planned today.

## KERCHIEF RELIEF

Well it ain't so funny
when my nose is red and runny
and the only nostril relief
is my spotted handkerchief
in which to quickly sneeze
thus preventing more disease,
but what else can I do
when I'm choked up, flue by flu?.

## DAY'S END

There's the sound of a paw
Scratching the door,
Then a beam of bright light
Breaks into the night
As my dog sprints by
In his corner to lie.
On closing the door
And making secure,
My duties are done
Contentment's begun.
Now gladly I retire
To my chair by the fire,
Where, in silence say
My thanks for the day.

## REPEAT PERSCRIPTION

Oh dear doctor what can I do
I believe I've got Parrot- Flue
The Doc' gave direction
To cure the infection
Keep repeating "pretty Polly loves you".

## DESPAIRING

Why does our dear Son now pose
in clothes fit for scaring crows
and walk about “Belsen” thin,
the answers bloody Heroin.
Now he seems to have lost the fight
to act the way he knows is right.
Some say he’s fuelled on Crack-Cocaine
the deadly stuff that warps the brain,
he sleeps rough, from place to place
and begs on streets without shame-face.
We wonder what else can be done
or have the drugs now finally won?.

## GRAIN OF TRUTH

Think not of things that have gone,
with hope, the future look on.
Enjoy every day that’s begun
before they bleach in the sun.
For present just like the past
to the desert marches fast,
there its fine granule to lay
amongst countless on display.

## LONELY HEARTS ADD

no ties
no lies
blue eyes
firm thighs
nice size
hair dyes
still tries
no cries
man wise
no disguise
prompt replies
needs t.l.c.
she sighs.

## SWEETHEART

I love you more than a little
I love you more than a lot
I love you more than anything
I love you with all I've got.

## OBSERVATION

So you want your money back
for the dress you've never worn,
although there's  faint soup stains
and the lace is slightly torn.
You say it doesn't suit you
and that it's rather tight,
but o how lovely you looked
at the "Hunt Ball" last night

## SECRET

I have a big secret
I'll never never tell,
O please! just me.
O K, ah well.
So she told the secret
and broke the spell,
now everyone knows
where the Unicorns dwell.

# WIFEY

I've written poems about flowers
and about those magnificent trees,
but I've never mentioned bow legs
Or my wife's knobbly knees.
I've joked about the weather
those ever changing skies,
yet I haven't discussed ever
my wife's wayward eyes.
I've even laughed at Ken Dodd's
noticeable bucked teeth
but mentioning my dear ones
would certainly bring me grief.
Sometimes I'm apt to admire
a girl with a smart figure,
though whcn my wife undresses
I try hard not to snigger.
I've talked about some weird things
that can be seen on Earth,
but to discuss my wife's anatomy,
is more than I am worth.

## MY PRECIOUS

How hard I've worked to make you bonnie
and keep you close by my side,
jealous that others may try to take you,
that's why your presence I  hide.
You alone fill my precious dreams
with you I can travel anywhere,
it's you who provides my food and shelter
and comforts me when things are hard to bear.
By my side you sleep, giving contentment
as I hold you lovingly by the hand,
and when I arise in the morning,
I pray my purse that you will expand.

## SIMMERING

Sitting calmly,
Waiting patiently,
Wondering casually,
Is it on time?

Getting restless,
Feeling helpless,
Being pointless,
If it is late.

Rising angrily,
Pacing quickly,
Muttering constantly,
Where's that damn train?

# FINAL PARTING
(VILLANELLE)

Do not flowers send
Throw them all away
If our love must end

Let us not pretend
You have gone astray
Do not flowers send

She was my best friend
And will surely pay
If our love must end

How do you intend
To try and save the day?
Do not flowers send

I strongly recommend
You leave without delay
As our love must end

On you I can't depend
Faithful you'll never stay
So no more flowers send
Now love's at an end.

# MAGPIE MILE

The Magpies they sit by and await
some other poor creatures fate,
getting flattened like a toad
as it crosses the busy road.

There to be flattened time and again
'till there's little that remains
like foxes, rabbits, hedgehogs too,
never a pretty site to view.

Soon the Magpies fly to feast
on the mince of the deceased,
ever watchful they don't expire
crushed beneath the tread of  tyre.

# JUST RACING AROUND

(FOR NEIL)

I'm rushing to nowhere in particular
and determined to get there fast,
my shiny car is my best friend
and we don't intend to be passed.
If someone tries to overtake us
I give the horn a quick blast
then put my foot to the floorboards
letting them see they're outclassed.

Now last night this car was following
and I got it into my mind
that I must show off my wheels
and leave this chancer behind.
Well I did my best to shake him,
doing ninety miles an hour,
but he came gliding past
with such graceful power.
It's only then that I realized
that I had better stop,
as bright lights flashed around,
for I'd raced the traffic cop.

## OBSERVATION TOWER

Heathrow Airport all-time bright,
twenty-four hours, planes in flight.
Flight-control keeps traffic flowing
observing all comings and goings.
There must be perfect timing
between arrivals and those climbing
high into the atmosphere
where from sight they disappear.
All that then can be seen
is their blip on the radar screen,
which is forever scanning
enabling flight control planning.

Without keen eyes, there would be
Aviation calamity.

## TAKE NOTICE

Picking your nose whilst on the loo
Is not a nice thing to do
And then to smear it on the wall
Shows you've no respect at all
So if you wish to dispose
Of the gunge up in your nose
Do not flick, smear or chew
Use a piece of soft tissue

## YELLOW SPEED BOX

I know you're waiting yellow box
may you and your owners be full of pox.
Cautiously now I watch my speed
so I'm not trapped by your greed.
Those close white markings on the ground
warn to late that you're around.
Alas, good drivers unsuspecting
through the post are collecting
fines and points because of you,
more harm than good that's what you do
suddenly winking your crafty eye,
"You dirty rotten traffic spy!"

## AFTERMATH

The intense heat,
Speed of movement,
Force of power,
Violent sounds,
Glowing colours,
Smell of sulpher,
Crackle of burning,
Fear for life,
All have gone,
only
Black lava rocks
remain.

# PAIN

There are questions in my mind that need answers,
Answers that I find do not appear,
Only visions brief that reveal my grief,
Which down my cheek brings another tear.

I want to know why he doesn't love me
After being so close for many years,
Kindling clear light through our children bright
Who's happiness knew no quarreling fears.

Photos bring back those precious memories
Of sunny summers spent on silver sand,
Together our happy faces seen in foreign places
Strolling so contented hand in hand.

There are questions in my mind seeking answers
Of thoughts that pierce me like a dart,
They say that time will heal the pain that I feel,
Until then, here bleeds a lonely heart.

## IN LOVE

I hear her voice
I see her face,
my thoughts are spent
in joys embrace.
I smell fine hair
I touch soft skin,
a body so firm
and pure within.
That perfect form
from head to toe,
no prettier flower
at Chelsea show.

## ALTERING THE CLOCKS

From his duty he will not cower
Though they put back the clocks an hour
At the sign of daybreak
Our old cock will awake
And renew his vocal power.

# THE PLASTIC TREE

I saw a plastic tree indoor
at a large department store,
everything was of proportional size,
the colours deceiving to the eyes.
But then I thought about our trees
their motion at the slightest breeze,
lifting and swaying to and fro
whichever way the winds may blow.
I thought of the sounds of falling rain
that refreshes all the leaves again.
The dawn chorus that can be heard
from the throat, of many a bird
perched upon the branches high
where the trees hide the sky.
I thought of our  trees in sunlight
and their silhouette's at night.
Then those words came to me,
"Only God could make a tree".

# PROBLEM SOLVED

My wife sent me to the supermarket
to buy food for our dog and cat,
she said, their meals must be delicious
but she didn't want her Lovelies to get fat.
I was shown the pet food sections
and I couldn't believe my eyes,
there was row after row of brands I didn't know
in packages of all shapes and size.
She'd insisted I read all the details
to make sure my choices were right,
but after three hours of reading
I decided I'd better take flight.
That night eager pets were eating
out of their own named dish,
one was eating my roast beef
and the other, her fresh tuna fish.

# 21/10/03

I am sixty-two once only
and my year started today,
I was sixty-one once only
but I don't regret it passing away.

I was twenty-one once only
and looking back I see
the things I would now change,
if time was left to me.

I was thirteen once only
just starting my teenage
when hopes were plentiful
and Doris Day the rage.

I was seven once only
and the eldest son,
that's when I realised
that life wasn't only fun.

I was one once only
my very first birthday,
O! how those many years
have swiftly flown away.

# THE BEACH

It's not in the sea
yet it's hardly on land.
It's either quite pebbly
or soft golden sand.
So wet and then dry
and the same over again,
that's how it has been
and  will always remain.

It's nice, to walk on
or play different sports,
a spot for relaxing
in costume or shorts.
The place all children
are  delighted to be,
just digging and paddling
at the side of the sea

# FROM A DISTANCE

I've turned off the Tele,
fed-up with the news of Iraq,
though they'll still be fighting
with challenge and counter attack.
There still will be the carnage,
and people filled with fear
not knowing what's happening
their future being unclear.
I think I'll walk in the garden,
in the warm springtime air
absorbing peace and beauty
that reflects everywhere.
Later, when I'm in the mood
I'll switch on the Tele again
to find out what's destroyed
and the problems that remain.
I'll note again the scores
of the wins and losses
brought to us from a safe place
by those brave battle bosses.

# THOUGHTS WHILST DRINKING FROM A PINK GOBLET OF ELDERBERRY WINE.

Picking Elderberries, I well remember
for the wine making last September.
now it's January and the bush is bare,
not a single leaf to be seen anywhere.

Come April time the bush will posses
lots of new leaves forming her dress,
next bouquets of flowers she will wear,
small, pinky-white, dappling everywhere.

Then as the months of summer come and go
the elderberries form and gradually grow
till once again they hang in their glory
the start of another wine making story.

So now I'll raise my goblet of Elderberry wine,
!To you and yours from me and mine!.

## GUESS WHO?

It is as before
only you I adore,
since that very first day
that love came my way.
So dearest Valentine,
"Forever be mine".

## POST SCRIPT

These aren't trite lines of verse
to say that "I love you",
for when we kiss and converse
you know my love is true.
These words come from deep inside
my strong-beating heart,
where love latent did abide
'till pierced by Cupids dart.

# MY BLACK TIE

This black tie hangs on its own
away from the colourful array of silk
and cotton ties in my wardrobe.
Unlike some of my ties, its shape and
material have never become unfashionable,
it has always been suitable for the
sad occasions that I have had to wear it.
My thoughts drift back now to some of
the sorrowful times that I have worn it
and dampened it with teardrops.
Those unexpected burials and cremations
of loved ones, family, friends and
colleagues from where I've worked.
Some deaths I have been prepared for
and been thankful that their lingering pain
was finally over, others were a shock
leaving me terribly saddened at times.
I know that one day I will be at a funeral
and for the first and last time I wont
be wearing this black tie.

# THE COASTAL HIKE
(VILLANELLE)

This black tie hangs on its own
away from the colourful array of silk
and cotton ties in my wardrobe.
Unlike some of my ties, its shape and
material have never become unfashionable,
it has always been suitable for the
sad occasions that I have had to wear it.
My thoughts drift back now to some of
the sorrowful times that I have worn it
and dampened it with teardrops.
Those unexpected burials and cremations
of loved ones, family, friends and
colleagues from where I've worked.
Some deaths I have been prepared for
and been thankful that their lingering pain
was finally over, others were a shock
leaving me terribly saddened at times.
I know that one day I will be at a funeral
and for the first and last time I wont
be wearing this black tie.

## A MILLION TO ONE CHANCE

What chances are there of success,
There's very little I confess.
As much as praying to the Moon
To change January into June.
More chance of catching a Whale
On a rod with a bent nail.
A better chance of becoming King
Or wearing the new Pope's ring.
A greater chance of walking on water
Or marrying a Pharaoh's daughter.
My chances of success it seems
Are more likely in my dreams.

## WORK OF ART

She walks along with poise and grace
silicone peaks, proud of place.
Hair well dyed to hide the grey,
Lippo-suction's taken away
fat thighs and enormous waist,
missing teeth have been replaced.
Plastic surgery's done its best,
fine cosmetics hide the rest.
Dressed up in the latest fashion
she's fighting nature with a passion.

## AT THIS MOMENT AS I WRITE

Boats are bobbing on the briny
Cars, cruising on carriageways
Trains travelling through tunnels
Flights flying in the firmament
People passing on pavements
And old Sam snoring on the settee.

# IN PURSUIT

I can catch a rabbit and hold it firm
though it tries to scratch and squirm.
I can catch a young frisky colt
before it gets the chance to bolt.
I can catch a chicken dodging by
even when it's started to fly.
I can catch fish in river and stream
whether large or small, pike or bream.
I can catch a fox on the prowl,
even a lonesome hooting owl.
but alas, though I really do try,
I never can catch love in your eye.

# COFFEE CUP

At my favorite café on the sea front at Agay (French Riviera)
Plain coffee cup, I wonder how many times you have
been filled and emptied this summer-season?.
How many times you have been washed and dried,
held in the left hand or the right?.
I wonder, how many different countries have people come
from who have sat down here and embraced you as they
have swallowed with pleasure and refreshment the
coffee from within your brim?.
Coffee cup, it matters not to me where you were made
or how much you cost, only that you now serve well your
purpose as I sit here in the sunshine,
looking contentedly out to sea.

## SURVIVOR

I've had more than my share
of the depths of despair
but now at last I'm free.
Yet still I will fight
with all my might
against any injustice I see.

I know how it feels
to reel from bad deals
and things tough as can be.
Thank God, I did cope
when there seemed no hope
and the devil hounded me.

I'm sure, now at last
I can handle the past
and forget bad company.
With nothing to hide
and love by my side
I can face life's destiny.

# BOUGHT AS SEEN

I have no tax
or M.O.T
the tyres are bold
no insurance fee.
The lights don't work
on the near side,
the doors won't lock
it's open wide.
The gearbox knocks,
the tracking's out.
There is no horn
I have to shout.
When it rains
it now leaks in
where the seals
had once bin.
The hand-brake's now
reached the top
I need a brick when I stop.
The engines tired
and losing oil,
the water leaks
and it starts to boil.
The bodywork's really poor
and it can't take filler no more.
So now, it's for sale
"Bought as seen",
lovingly described
in the Add-magazine.

# IN OUR GARDEN

Daffodil's in full bloom
they nod and gently sway,
how beautiful the show
on this delightful day.

The snowdrops have withered
without leaving a clue
of how charming they
were, carpeting the view.

Sweet scent of hyacinths
now waft through the air,
their multicoloured presence
adding splendour everywhere.

Sadly, crocuses are fading
after such a fine display,
but time marches on
and they must slip away.

Soon the wild bluebells
will joyously appear,
proclaiming to all
that summertime is near.

# WHAT HAPPENED?

How did she become a Druggie
with so little flesh on the bone
and clothes so scruffy and smelly
that a scarecrow wouldn't own.

When did she get the desire
that's turned into a crave,
making heroin the master
and her a dutiful slave.

I guess she wanted to be merry
with her mates at the dance,
and someone handed out pills,
so she took one, just by chance.

From there she popped more pills
to get the same effect,
doing it very discreetly
so no-one would suspect.

Next she tried soft drugs
'till they had no effect,
so on to deadly heroin
which, now she has to inject.

Sadly, she cares about nothing
except, trying to make a score,
those words, "respect" and "love"
don't matter to her anymore.

# LONESOME DOVE
(A RESPONSE TO A POEM)

Tiny timid lonesome dove
chooses not to fly
though the sun is up above
in a clear blue sky.

Tiny timid lonesome dove
O please tell me why,
you no longer coo
only hide and cry?

Tiny timid lonesome dove
sobbing, makes reply,
"I miss my dear cousins
who are now Pigeon-pie.

# SELF DEFENCE

The stranger came rushing towards me,
shouting what he was going to do,
his looks were really angry
but for why, I hadn't a clue.
I gripped my teeth, clenched my fist
whilst looking him in the eye,
waiting for that moment
when both my fists must fly.
It's not something that I wanted
deep down inside to do,
but that strong primeval voice
Cried "protection now for you".

# GET THE MESSAGE

Drugs cost money
and what is more
if you are addicted
you'll always be poor.
You'll steal or sell
and crawl in the slime,
to feed your addiction
you'll commit any crime.
Addicts will never
achieve any goal,
they're like square pegs
in life's round hole.
If you never start
you never need stop
or risk becoming
a poor social flop.
It is oh so easy
So easy to start,
but just try stopping
you'll bleed from the heart.

# JUST RETIRED

Let me bring to your attention
(no more enslaved-by-convention)
the joys of being free
from the constraints that fettered me.
Each morning, I can now arise
without the tiredness in my eyes,
or aching muscles, flesh rubbed sore,
hardships never mentioned before.
It's time at last for me to pursue
the thoughts of things I've wanted to do.
No point in leaving deeds too late
for, who knows the hand of fate
what great times it may bring
or misfortunes final sting.

## WHAT!

If I became rich and famous
the first thing I think I'd do
is dispose of my dear old wife
and have a young piece twenty-two.

But alas, I've only dreamed about it,
really thinking the whole thing through,
the things we'd do during the night
means that I'd need replacing too.

## AFTER CHRISTMAS

I've decided to go on a detox
and leave all those choc's in the box
though it's all very fine
to wine and to dine
I now struggle to put on my socks.

Now I really have to admit
that my waistline has stretched a bit
shall I try to get slim?
training hard at the gym
or buy some new trousers that fit?

After all that is said and done
I must resist every cream bun
and all those sweets so nice
I will have to think twice
or my battle will never be won

## CHRISTMAS TIME

There's them that have got
And those who have not
Like all Christmases before,
And those that want peace
And turmoil to cease,
Whilst others cry out for war.

But at Christmas I know
As the years quickly go,
They cannot be repeated.
So lets dance and sing
And enjoy everything,
Until the year's completed.

## CONTINUANCE

The known limit is passed,
bells ring in the New Year.
Time still ticks on as fast
with all its hopes and fears.
And  having crossed that line
we continue to tell the tale,
hopeful our health remains fine
and good fortune doesn't fail.

## RESOLUTION!

I'll put myself on trial
with a bit of self denial
and hope that my fasting
will the months be outlasting,
'till I am somewhat thinner
than this bloated beginner.
For I  have had enough
of all that fattening stuff
at Christmas and New Year,
which, now I must steer clear.

## SOAKED

A scared ladd'ie stood by the door
Watching a terrific downpour'
He said, it's so fright'ning
This thunder and light'ning
And my trousers aren't dry anymore.

## INTEMPERANCE

Now my intemperance has been
To eat lots of sweets in-between
Each delicious meal
And whenever I feel
My desiring for food is keen.

## HEART OF ENGLAND
(CRYTOGRAPH)

Ilfracombe
Tenby

Ipswich
Sudbury

York
Odham
Ullswater

Tamworth
Harlow
Abingdon
Torquay

Ipswich

Lincoln
Ormskirk
Vale of Pickering
Easingwold.

## PROGRESS ?

To me it wouldn't be a surprise
if they tried to categorise
not only your weight
and physical state
but also the smile in your eyes.

## SOME UNKNOWN TOMB

There is a silent place
that never sees a face,
a small area of its own
of which nought is known.
And so it will remain
unaffected by sun and rain.
A space void of sin,
no pollutants within.
A nature's sealed spot
that mankind forgot.

## THE HORSESHOE RING

To me it wouldn't be a surprise
if they tried to categorise
not only your weight
and physical state
but also the smile in your eyes.

# BRITAINS GLORY

Oh, To be in England
one of our great poets said,
though from wintry weather
he had long since fled.
Other poets like Byron
sought refuge o'er the sea
but their hearts still remained
amongst England's greenery.
Now Hardy wrote of Dorset
and Wordsworth of the lakes
whilst Masefield sang of the sea
where wave on wave breaks.
Our Robbie wrote of the Highlands
and so did Sir Walter Scot
whilst Dylan wrote of Wales
its beauty he ne'er forgot.
Our island has its seasons
and their glory can be seen
whether dressed in a gown of snow
or clothed in summer green.
So lovely is the countryside
from vale to mountain view
inspiring poets for centuries
and our finest artists to.

## PATCHES

I have a patch to stop me smoking
and a patch to stop the drink,
one to abort my gambling
and to change the way I think.
I've a patch to reduce my eating
large amounts of delicious food,
A patch to prevent exhibitioning
and waking up in the nude.
Now I've acquired a master patch
That's going to take control
but I'm not sure of instructions
it just says "Cover the hole".

## EPITAPH TO NORAH

To earths cell herself confined
when aching body, tired mind
decide to leave the crowd behind.
Now she's got blessed release
from the pains that never cease.
Sleep at last, o perfect peace.

## FROM WORDS TO WAR

But, she said
ah! he replied,
then he countered
which she denied,
again she accused,
he stepped aside
quickly retorting
though hurting inside.
Then new tactics
are quickly applied,
few words now
as hearts collide.

## LIMERICK

A sexy young tart called Heather
tried washing her clothes of leather
she said, all's gone wrong
I've shrunk the dam thong
now it wont fit nowhere, not ever

# SPECIAL OFFERS

(Villanelle)

That’s just right for me
When the bright signs say.
“Buy one get one free”.

From sprays to packet tea,
Providing everything’s Ok.
That’s just right for me.

I don’t think it’s trickery
Having a nice display.
”Buy one get one free”

Whilst stores guarantee
Their word on fair-play,
That’s just right for me.

It’s good economy
According to surveys
“Buy one get one free”

Now I’ve a family
Where costs interplay,
So, that’s just right for me.
“Buy one get one free”.

## ROUNDABOUT

I stopped my car and asked a man
if he could direct me to Dover street,
he smiled at me and said he can,
his directions I now repeat.
You go left at the next lights
and follow until you meet
a church on your far right
that's the start of Martin street.
Go down it till the very end
then your journey will be complete,
and you will be back herc my friend
on the opposite side of the street.

## OUR MAURICE

My brother got his tan in Africa
out on the big game shoots,
whilst I got mine in Nottingham
from a counter down at Boots.

## REFLECTIONS

The new Pizza Hut was full
and McDonalds was busy again,
whilst there paused I
a sad penniless guy
with shoes letting in the rain.

# MISS-TIMED

Hears my thoughts upon the page
About one morning's road rage,
How my car got wiped out
On the King's Mill roundabout.

I was indicating where to go
Approaching the island fairly slow,
When suddenly into view
Came a car charging through.

Quickly he began to break
On realising his mistake,
As there wasn't room to pass
Not even across the grass.

Suddenly the bloody thing
Collided with my right wing,
Causing my car to veer
Without any chance to steer.

So I finished up hitting a post
All shook-up white as a ghost.
Car no longer fit to ride
My wife crying by my side.

Anger welled from deep inside
I was going to thrash his hide,
But on seeing the injuries he'd got
All my anger I soon forgot.

Sorrow came as anger went
On seeing to what extent,
The harm that his error had done
Someone there had lost a son.

Since that day whenever I see
Drivers acting recklessly,
Brings to mind that young man's fate
Brought about through being late.

## HOOKED ON HEROIN

Once they hear the name
In their brain repeated,
Things are not the same
All their hopes defeated.

No longer do they care
About morals they have known,
All is in the air,
Every principle has flown.

They will beg and steal
Just to get their fix,
Such contempt they reveal
Through their dirty tricks.

## LIMERICK

Sue wanting her lips to look plump
tried everything including a pump
Her mate said have no fear
I've got a good idea
and gave her a bloody good thump.

# FREAK STORMS

Where clear water laps and the Black-gull flaps
along the rocky shore,
there's where wrecks of mighty oak decks
have littered the ocean floor.
Many a night that's foul when driving winds howl
have brought tars misery,
as they've tried to steer their vessels clear
of the jaws of destiny.
There's many a heart fails in the roar of the gales
as riggings all break free,
and not much hope for masters to cope
against the devil's ferocity.

## PROGRESS

The old Texas wildcatter
Reminisced of day's gone by
Of wooden framed Derricks
And crude oil gushing high
Whil'st the young offshore driller
Spoke of new technology
In blowout prevention
And wellheads under the sea

## Gusting 90

He could hear the winds howling
Sense the bitter cold
And feel the motion of the barge as it heaved about.
Pounded by the charging waves that raced onward,
Towards the distant grey rim.

Aloft, the masthead flapped frantically
And the windsock kept losing its sense of direction.

Nearby on top of a swaying pole,
The anemometer spun round like the clubs of a crazy juggler
Whilst below, the pelting rain bounced off the deck
And the crane cab where he sat
peering out through steamy windows,
Out onto the stormy scene.

# THE PRICE OF OIL

The Sea Quest rides upon the waves,
Searching the North Sea for oil.
All day and all night, its engines hum,
And rigmen strenuously toil.
Way high up in the derrick,
The pipes swing to and fro,
Whilst the oilmen work incessantly
On the rigfloor down below.
You can hear the clash of steel
And the squealing of the brake,
See the roughnecks' dash about,
There's a connection to make.
Two men stand by the tongs
And one man goes to stab,
He swings the pipe across the deck
And makes the sudden jab.
Then smartly the big tong's
Round the pipes are clasped,
There's a squealing and a screeching
As steel to steel is grasped,
Next goes on the kelly
And the pipes spin round and round,
Whilst far below mud circulates
And the bit bites into the ground.

It's a tough life on an oilrig
And very dangerous too,
Whether you be a crane driver,
Or one of the drilling crew.
So next time you buy your petrol,
Or wonder at the price of oil,
Remember that on the oilrigs,
In all weathers, men have to toil.

(BP Seaquest was the most famous oil rig in the story of North Sea Oil. The Seaquest's greatest achievement was when she located BP's Forties Field in 1970 she also discovered the Andrew Field 4 years later)

## ON STREAM

This once was a new location
Just a patch on the North Sea swell.
And all was young and exciting,
As we began to spud, in the first well.
But the exploration days are all over,
The last appraisal well has been drilled,
And the experts have done calculating
How many barrels per day can be filled.

And the excitement of the game has ended
As the numerous platforms appear
What once was a thrilling experiment
Is just normal procedure this year.

## Ode To The S.S.V. Uncle John "Divers".

A hundred and fifty metres below the surface
Of the cold and treacherous North Sea,
Divers are working day and night
For the benefit of you and me.
They work in dangerous conditions
Where little can be seen,
Amidst the dark and murky waters
Where man has never been.
They connect and weld the pipelines
Like engineers on the land,
Except there's a world of a difference
A hundred and fifty metre below on the sand.

# RETURNING

From all around the globe
They picked the drilling crew
Some are old hands at the game
To some excitingly new.

Travelling by all forms of transport,
They arrive in old Aberdeen
For the early morning check in,
On route to the North Sea scene.

Patiently they sit at the airport
Waiting for the Sunburgh flight
Some are tired through travelling,
Others with drinking into the night.

It's an hour's flight to Sunburgh
Where as usual there's delay
Which could be for several hours
Or maybe they're stranded the day.

This creates a feeling of depression
Which shows midst the restless crew,
Each face marked with expression
After hours with nothing to do

For if there's one thing dreaded by oilmen
Which they find really hard to bear,
It's landing at Sunburgh airport
And then getting stranded there

Eventually the flight is announced
And they soar from the aerodrome
Filled with the thoughts of work
And thoughts of those back home

Soon they will be landing
Their travelling finally done
And one more cycle completed
Another one just begun

# ROUGHNECKS

They sleep, work and bide their time
Till they return ashore,
Leaving behind the sweat and grime
For the life they love the more.
For some work means a brand new car
To others a place of their own,
Whilst there are those who travel afar,
To places they'd never have known.

Now some men save for a rainy day,
Respecting the money they earn.
Whilst some, their pay they fritter away
With not the slightest concern.
And the way some choose, to gamble and lose,
You'd think they'd money to burn.

# Brent At Night

Beneath the platforms gaily lit
Each an isle of clustered light,
The heaving waves swirl and leap
Revealed in the depth of night.

Whilst above, the clouds go sailing by
All tinged with the rosy glow,
That reflects in variant brilliance
With the raging flares below.

And the surrounding boats and barges,
Add to the amazing sight,
As they move in all directions
With mast lights beaming bright.

# GORDIE BROOKES THE UNION MAN

Gordie Brookes was a Postman
In old Sutton Town.
He said "Brothers you can
put your mailbags down".
Today we go on strike
to protect present conditions,
so park up your bikes,
"we'll suffer no attrition!".
Brothers we have no choice
or a stranglehold they'll gain,
and no longer will we have a voice,
just a "Ball And Chain".
"Progress" the Management shout,
It's just a new working way,
But Posties know what it's all about.
Longer hours and shorter pay.

# MY FRIEND

No more will he turn again the pages
of old books that he loved so much,
nor dwell on certain lines for ages,
well worn by hands of tender touch.
Bookmarks remain in places which remind
of favorite poems he knew by heart,
those lovely sonnets now I find
bring closeness though we're spheres apart.

How I miss the presence of his smile
at haunts where we used to meet,
the speed of life would slow awhile
in conversations, serious and sweet.
But all that now is at an end
And I sadly miss my life-long friend.

# FEARS EXPOSED

When I'm alone, why must you haunt
and with bad memories cruelly taunt
of times I wish to leave behind
to the shredder of the mind.
Yet, still I tremble with fear
When lifelike you reappear.
Reality tells me you have gone
and that the years have marched on
to better times than I had known
when flesh was sparse upon the bone.
Those beatings! Time and time again
disturb the peace within my brain,
O! how I've prayed, that "living hell"
would finally leave the last brain cell.
Now, I must recount each dreadful scene
in Crown Court from behind a screen.

# THE OLD WATER MILL

Pat was wandering alone
amidst ever delighting sights
making all cares take flight,
singing her favourite song
about the joy that is found
when new love comes around.

She was absorbingly unaware
as she paused by the stream
relishing a lover's dream,
that someone else was there,
until just by chance
she gave a backward glance.

There to her great joy,
walking through the grass
where the Roe deer pass,
was her darling boy.
Waving arms, delighted
at being once more united.

Soon in that quiet place
where brown trout leap
and barn owls sleep,
they tenderly embrace;
letting the world go by
without a question why.

# GUIDING LIGHT

With you by my side, we travel along,
sharing all, whatever it may be,
passing through, clouded or starlit nights
over calm or restless sea.

With you by my side through the days,
there's warmth though cold winds may blow,
a shelter from that strong noon-day sun
whose rays search out places they go.

With you by my side we have the strength
to surmount obstacles along life's way,
comforted by a joy that's ever strong,
Support at all times, without delay.

With you by my side, life is full,
the part that means most is always there,
that ever-glowing beacon called love
which shines on lovers everywhere.

With you by my side till life's end,
that's how we want it to be,
then on and on, maybe together?
through those veils of eternity.

# A MOTHERS DILEMMA

Now what can I get her for Christmas
a present she hasn't got,
something that will really please her
but won't be costing a lot.
She's got games for her computer
and a new dryer for her hair,
Shoes, she's got so many
that never will get any wear.
Dresses fill all her wardrobe
I can hardly close the door,
girl's clothes I used to buy her
she refuses to wear any more.
Last Christmas I bought her a watch
one of the trendy kind
she wore it once to a party
came home and left it behind.
So I think I'll get her gift vouchers
to spend at the new Asda store
that way she gets what she chooses,
Now! That's a problem no more.

## CAPTURED IN TIME

There's a painting in the gallery
wherein three children play,
enjoying the bright sunshine
around about midday.
Those healthy little faces
filled with springtime charms
haven't the slightest idea
of future's many alarms.
So here they remain, captured,
More than two centuries on
though like their fine surroundings,
To dust, they've long since gone.

## FED UP!

I wish that I had got a better audience
than this one that's half-asleep,
one that looked more enthusiastic
and not so glum.
I wish that I had a better audience
that looked interested in me
and wanted to spend some time with me
not one whose eyes keep twitching.
I wish I had a better audience
that didn't look as though
it hadn't had a wash since yesterday.
But alas, I cannot shave without my mirror.

# OUTCLASSED

It was high noon and I thought
that I was ready for the challenge,
my sporting weapon was loaded
and ready for the task ahead.
I knew before I started that
there could only be one winner,
just one last look at the areas
the judges would be scoring on.
The areas were as follows,
creativity, impact, craftmanship,
voice, and form structure.
I studied the criteria paying very
close attention, then nervously
I put my fountain pen back in its case.

# MAKING A RESERVATION
(INTRODUCTION)

In Nice on the French Riviera there is a hotel of
world renown called the Hotel Negresco
where the rich and famous go to stay.
It's a fabulous place filled with wonderful
antiques and priceless works of art.
Bill Gates the computer billionaire offered
the lady owner a blank cheque if she would sell
the Negreso to him, but she politely refused his invitation.
When the old doorman at the Negresco retired,
it is rumoured that he had become a millionaire
on the tips that he made as the doorman.

My little poetical sketch is about a simple
fellow who hasn't a clue about how the other-half lives,
he's just arrived in Nice and he is using his
mobile phone to try and find somewhere to stay.

# MAKING A RESERVATION

(Sketch)

(Snatches of a one way conversation on his mobile)

Hello, is that the Negresco Hotel,
It's Clivey Brookes here,

Nooooo, that's not my Rolls'
I'm on a coach parked near.

I'd like to stay for awhile
and then treat me-self to a beer

Nooooo, I don't want champagne
and I think caviar tastes queer.

So there's only grand suites available,
and what was that price ye say!

Well I only wanted bed and breakfast
for a couple of nights and a day.

I hope the mattress is comfy
and there's clean sheets on the bed,
Cos I once slept away for a football match
and came home with fleas in me head.

Nooooo, I haven't a bankers card
nor cheques or plastic trash,
I always pays me money
and only deals in cash.

What! I can't believe me ears,
no beef burgers and chips for lunch!
I think I'll try somewhere else
and gu to McDonald's to munch.

## THE COMMITTEE

We are a band of Back-Scratchers,
we all pee in one pot.
Over principles we don't argue,
all morals we've long forgot.
When it comes to money
scruples we certainly have not,
any signs of honey
all sit down to plot
and if folks complain
we don't give a jot!

We are a band of Back-Scratchers,
A VERY NASTY LOT!.

## SPRING BLOOM

Lips, soft touch that maiden fair
and let them roam everywhere,
hands, gently seek and caress
that beautiful form you now posses.
Eyes feast yourself and in your brain
let her perfect image remain,
thereby giving a chance to capture
that moment of springtime rapture

## HEART BROKEN

Why did it have to end so badly
leaving me filled with despair,
thinking in my heart, sadly
that you didn't really care.
When I see you now by chance
instantly I hurt inside
by that chemistry called romance
which blossomed then suddenly died.

Who knows, maybe someday?
love wont hurt as it does now.
Time seems to have a healing way,
and young memories somehow
become sweeter as they mature.
But loves pangs "I need no more"!

## BRITISH

I've read the poems of Kipling
and Henry Newbold too,
with feelings of admiration
for their patriotic view.
But how this country's changed
from the way those fathers planned,
no more the British Empire
or control of foreign lands.

Now, we are a breed
of multinational race,
who now live as one
wherever there's a place.
We're proud to be British
whatever our colour or creed
and grateful to democracy
for the good life that we lead.

# SNOWED IN

I'm waiting for the Weeping Willow
to sprout its tufts of green,
I'm longing to see the Snowdrops
followed by the yellow scene
of Daffodils and Cowslips
along the old tow path,
after the cold March winds
have finally spent their wrath.
I'm thinking now of Bluebell time
what beauty then is seen,
Just one continuous carpet
around and in-between
those ancient great Oaks
with their canopies of green.
Oh the joy of summertime
travelling the waterways,
with the one that I love,
On long hot sunny days.
But now I must wait patiently
for the deep snow to thaw
before I dare venture
far from my cottage door.

# AGAIN

Again it's Sunday morning and I'm in a terrible state
After drinking too much and staying out late,
My face is badly bruised and my bones all ache,
While my poor head keeps throbbing as if it's going to break.
My mouth tastes awful and I just can't eat,
In fact it's taking all my time just to stay on my feet,
The state of my clothes say I must have had a fall
But my mind is a blank and there's nothing I recall.
Yet, although I'm feeling sorry I realise it serves me right,
For I know I shouldn't drink so much and stay out half the night.
Now I'm going to make my pledge, like so many times before,
This is the final time; "I'm going to drink no more!"

## SOMETHING DIFFERENT

Two lions met in a clearing
Each to prove his supremacy,
And they called to an onlooking buzzard
To judge who the champion must be.
So the buzzard approached each lion,
Explaining the rules to begin,
And with the wink of an eye, he whispered,
That the other couldn't possibly win.
Well, fiercely fought the brave lions
Till the last of their blood flowed free,
Then the buzzard announced his decision
As he flew to the ground for his tea.

# TO MY DEAR SON

Dear son, on your first birthday
These are the prayers I pray,
That the good lord will always be with you
Each night and every day.
God grant that you will grow up.
With the wisdom of the wise,
The health of an athlete
And yet, realise,
Some people are less fortunate
And have not strength of mind,
Or have some other affliction,
To them, always be kind.
Appreciate at all times
God's gifts to you at birth,
For surpassing all the riches
That man creates on earth.
Finally, god grant to you compassion
And understanding too.
Real peace and contentment
That lasts your whole life though.

## LIFE'S VOYAGE

Every emotion you feel
Forms part of a chart,
From the very beginning
To the last beat of your heart,
And life is as changeable
As the weather at sea,
Sometimes peaceful and calm
Or as rough as can be,
And the length of one's voyage
Is, to a certain degree,
Determined by the way
You sail on life's Sea.

## PINNACLES

So love, as steeples to heaven aspires,
Yet time may affect those architect's desires,
Though with the best intensions they conspire
To raise straight and true, Higher and higher,
For sometimes warp and shrinkage may be dire
And make a twisted point like Chesterfields' spire.

## IN TIME

There will be beautiful summers I'll never see
And new springs I'll never know,
There will be falling autumn leaves
Followed by the winters snow,
And the seas will advance and retreat
As the tides edd and flow to the shores,
Like they have done for thousands of years,
So continuing for thousands more,
And the mystical beauty of night
Will continue to follow the day,
Unless man, by his error, fights
And wipes his existence away.

## JEWELS

Alas we have these things
That are bartered for souls
And thrones of Kings
Who's magic can make a poor man rich
And their loss a rich man poor
These shiny jingling things bewitch
Both the evil and the pure.

## BOUNDEN DUTY

Some say it's not the time
some say it's not the place,
whilst some think that it's a disgrace;
but we're doing it.

Some think it's a crime
some think it's a shame
and we're not playing the game;
but we're pursuing it.

Now, we feel sometime
that we must see through
what our duty tells us to do;
though were ruing it.

## LIMERICK

A cunning old codfish named Fred
Watched the net nearing then fled.
For it wasn't his wish,
To end up in a dish,
With breadcrumbs right up to his head.

## THE THREE Ts

Too late
Too bad
Tough!.

# HOOK LINE AND SINKER

She tempted me, I took the bait
now I suffer the fish's fate,
though I tried to slip the hook
By every means in the book.
I wriggled, snatched and turned about
but could not get the grapple out.
I skipped the surface, dived below
using every fishy trick I know;
with not a flinch from tail to head
I even pretended to be dead.
Still, I landed in the proverbial net,
one bite to many I'll long regret.

So cleverly do some girls conceal
all the signs of rod and reel.